SOUTH AFRICA
‹THE BEAUTIFUL LAND›

SOUTH AFRICA
‣ THE BEAUTIFUL LAND ‣

Text by David Bristow

STRUIK

Struik Publishers (Pty) Ltd
(a member of The Struik Publishing Group (Pty) Ltd)
Cornelis Struik House
80 McKenzie Street
Cape Town
8001

Reg. No.: 54/00965/07

First published 1990
Second impression 1992
Third impression 1993
Fourth impression 1994
Fifth impression 1996

PHOTOGRAPHIC CREDITS
Gerald Cubitt: p.72 (top & bottom); p.73; p.74; p.75 (top); p.76/77; p.78 (top); p.79; p.80
Rob d'Alessandro: p.26 (bottom right)
Roger de la Harpe: p.16 (centre & bottom); p.17 (centre); p.71 (bottom)
John Haigh: p.12 (top); p.13 (bottom); p.19 (left)
Raymonde Johannesson: p.53 (bottom left)
Roy Johannesson: p.12 (centre & bottom)
Walter Knirr: cover; p.1; p.2/3; p.6/7; p.10/11; p.13 (centre); p.14 (top & centre); p.15 (top, centre & bottom); p.16 (centre); p.17 (top & bottom); p.18; p.20; p.21 (bottom); p.22 (top); p.23; p.24/25; p.26 (top); p.28; p.30; p.31; p.32; p.34; p.35; p.36/37; p.38; p.39; p.40 (top & bottom); p.42; p.43; p.44 (top & bottom); p.45; p.46/47; p.58; p.59; p.60 (top); p.61; p.62; p.63 (top & bottom); p.64/65; p.66; p.67; p.68; p.69
Peter Magubane: p.14 (bottom)
Peter Pickford: p.5; p.19 (right & top right); p.26 (bottom left); p.27 (left & right); p.29 (bottom); p.33 (left & right); p.48; p.49 (top & bottom); p.50 (top & bottom); p.51; p.52; p.53 (top & bottom right); p.54 (top & bottom); p.55 (top & bottom); p.56/57; p.60 (bottom); p.70 (top & bottom)
Janek Szymanowski: p.16 (top); p.71 (top)
Keith Young: p.21 (top); p.22 (bottom); p.29 (top); p.75 (bottom); p.78 (bottom)

Layout by Joan Sutton Design Studio c.c.
Typesetting by Hirt & Carter (Pty) Ltd, Cape Town
Reproduction by Unifoto (Pty) Ltd, Cape Town
Printed and bound by Kyodo Printing Co (Singapore) Pte. Ltd

ISBN 1 86825 068 7

FRONTISPIECE Protea cynaroides –
*South Africa's national flower and one
of the showiest blooms in the Cape
Floral Kingdom. This was one of the
first of the Cape flowers 'discovered' by,
and which so delighted, early European
naturalists with its beauty.*

PREVIOUS PAGE *The classic view of
Cape Town and Table Mountain. This
is the sight that has greeted sea-weary
sailors down the ages and which
prompted the 16th century
circumnavigator Sir Francis Drake
to declare it 'the fairest cape in all
the circumference of the world'.*

OPPOSITE *A family of cheetahs. These
elegant hunters are the fastest sprinting
land animals. They hunt, not by stealth
as do lions and leopards, but by speed
alone. They are often to be seen sitting
on top of termite mounds, scanning
the veld for prospective prey.*

OVERLEAF *The Eastern Transvaal is
a fertile land, rich in legend and tales
of adventure. It was in this area that
the country's first gold rush occurred,
predating the richer strikes on the
Witwatersrand. Holiday accommodation abounds and even sophisticated
hotel/time-share complexes such
as Mount Sheba, seen here in the
middleground, retain the
old-fashioned charm of the area.*

PAGES 10 & 11 *The moist montane
conditions and subtropical climate
along the eastern escarpment of South
Africa create ideal conditions for the
country's new but flourishing tea
industry.*

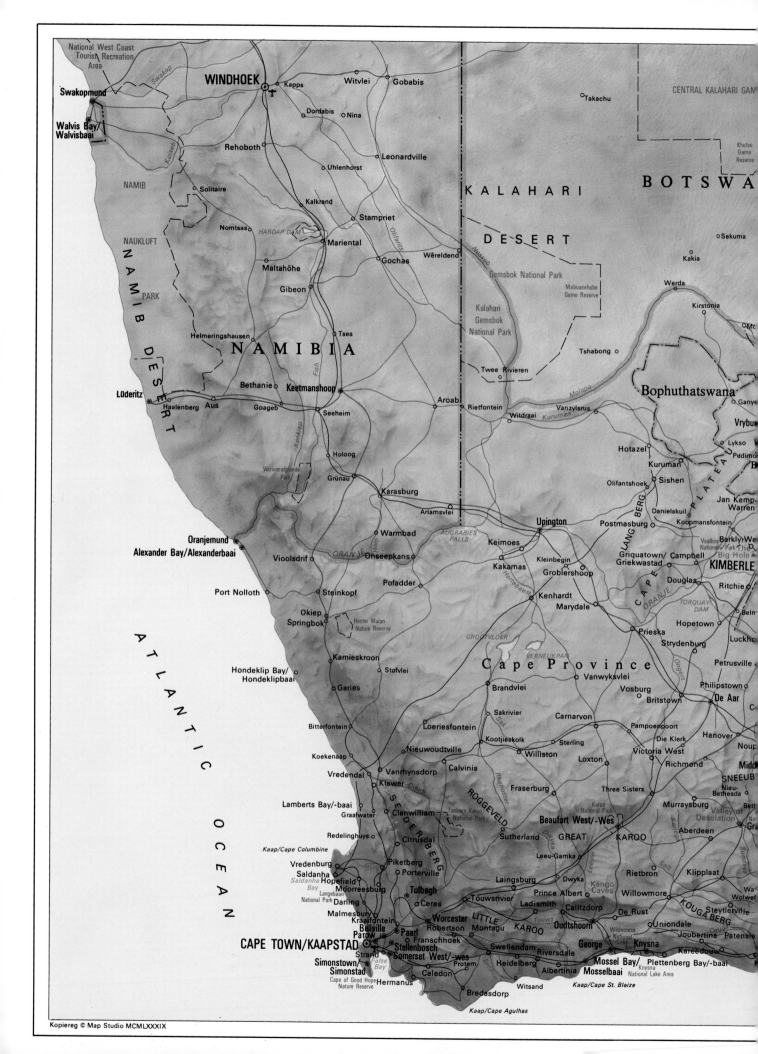

National West Coast Tourist Recreation Area

Swakopmund

Walvis Bay/ Walvisbaai

WINDHOEK Kapps Witvlei Gobabis

CENTRAL KALAHARI GAM

Takachu

Dordabis Nina

NAMIB Solitaire

Rehoboth

Uhlenhorst Leonardville

Khutse Game Reserve

NAUKLUFT Kalkrand

BOTSWA

Nomtsas Stampriet

K A L A H A R I

Maltahöhe HARDAP DAM Mariental

Wêreldend

Sekuma

D E S E R T

Kakia

PARK Gibeon Gochas

Gemsbok National Park

Werda

NAMIB Tses

Mabuasehube Game Reserve

Kirstonia

Helmeringshausen

N A M I B I A

Kalahari Gemsbok National Park

Tshabong

DESERT Bethanie Keetmanshoop

Twee Rivieren

Bophuthatswana

Lüderitz Aus Goageb

Haalenberg Seeheim

Aroab Rietfontein Vanzylsrus

Vrybu

Witdraai Kuruman

Molopo

Lykso Pudimo

Holoog

Hotazel

Vissrivierafgronde Park

Grünau

Olifantshoek Sishen

Kuruman

Jan Kemp Warren

Karasburg

Ariamsvlei

Upington Postmasburg Koopmansfontein Danielskuil

PLATEAU

KIMBERLE

Warmbad AUGRABIES FALLS Keimoes

Kleinbegin

Griquatown/ Campbell

Vaalbos Barkly We

The Big Hole

Oranjemund Vioolsdrif Onseepkans

Kakamas Groblershoop

Griekwastad

Douglas

Ritchie

Alexander Bay/Alexanderbaai ORANJE

ORANJE

BERG

CAPE

Pofadder Kenhardt

Herbeest

Prieska

Belm

Port Nolloth Steinkopf

Marydale

Hopetown

Luckho

TORQUAY DAM

Okiep Hester Malan Nature Reserve

GROOTVLOER

Strydenburg

Springbok

Onges

Petrusville

Kamieskroon Stofvlei

VERNEUKPAN

C a p e   P r o v i n c e

Philipstown

Hondeklip Bay/ Hondeklipbaai

Vanwyksvlei

Vosburg

De Aar

Garies

Brandvlei

Britstown

Co

A T L A N T I C Bitterfontein

Sakrivier Carnarvon

Pampoenpoort

Hanover

Noup

Loeriesfontein

Sak

Die Klerk

Victoria West

Midd

Koekenaap Nieuwoudtville Kootjieskolk Sterling Williston Loxton Richmond

SNEEUB

Nieu-Bethesda

Vredendal Vanrhynsdorp Calvinia

Rhenoster

Fraserburg

Three Sisters

Murraysburg

Valley of Desolation

Beth

Klawer Doorn

ROGGEVELD

Karoo National Park

O C E A N Lamberts Bay/-baai Graafwater Clanwilliam

CEDERBERG

Tankwa Karoo National Park

Beaufort West/-Wes

KAROO Aberdeen

Gra

Redelinghuys Citrusdal

Sutherland GREAT

Leeu-Gamka

Kaap/Cape Columbine

Piketberg

Dwyka

Rietbron Klipplaat

Vredenburg Porterville

Laingsburg

Kango Caves

Wa

Wolwel

Saldanha Hopefield Moorreesburg

Prince Albert Willowmore

Steytlerville

Saldanha Bay Darling

Tulbagh Ceres Touwsrivier Ladismith Calitzdorp De Rust

Uniondale

KOUGA BERG

Langebaan National Park

Dwars

Wilderness National Lake Area Joubertina Patensie

Malmesbury Kraaifontein Worcester LITTLE Montagu Oudtshoorn Towns

Bellville Paarl Robertson KAROO George Knysna Kareedouw

CAPE TOWN/KAAPSTAD Parow Franschhoek Swellendam Riversdale Knysna National Lake Area

Stellenbosch Somerset West/-wes Heidelberg Albertinia **Mossel Bay/**

Simonstown/ Strand Protem **Mosselbaai** **Plettenberg Bay/-baai**

Simonstad False Bay Caledon

Cape of Good Hope Nature Reserve Hermanus Witsand Kaap/Cape St. Blaize

Bredasdorp

Kaap/Cape Agulhas

Kopiereg © Map Studio MCMLXXXIX

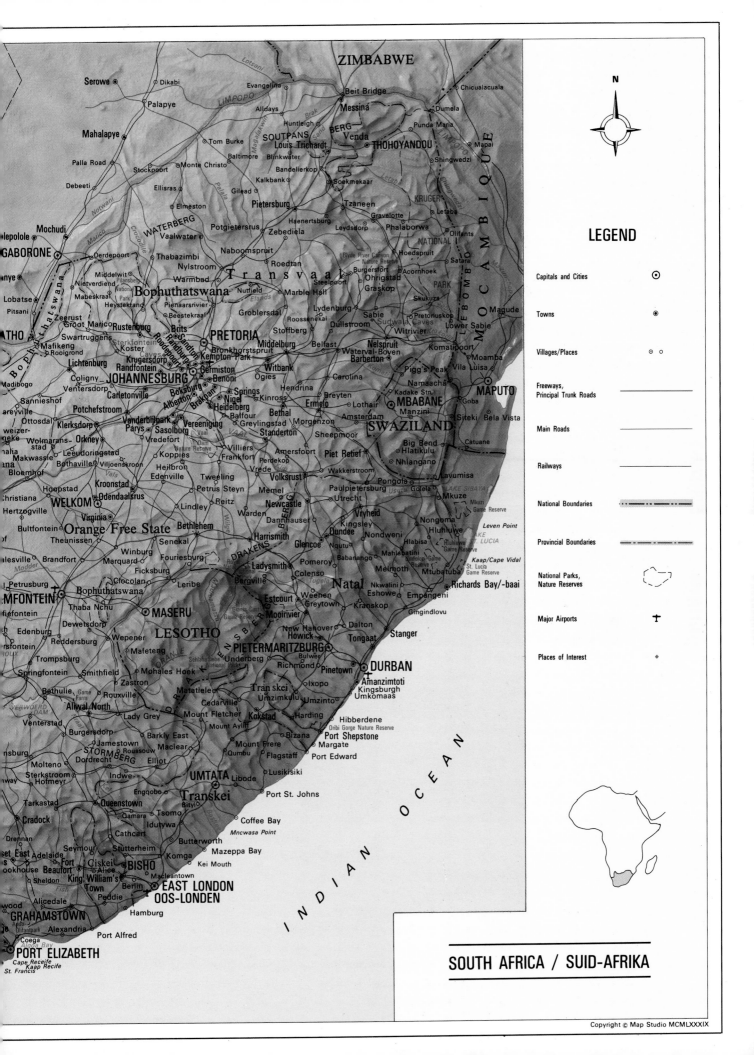

SOUTH AFRICA / SUID-AFRIKA

LEGEND

Capitals and Cities

Towns

Villages/Places

Freeways,
Principal Trunk Roads

Main Roads

Railways

National Boundaries

Provincial Boundaries

National Parks,
Nature Reserves

Major Airports

Places of Interest

Copyright © Map Studio MCMLXXXIX

INTRODUCTION

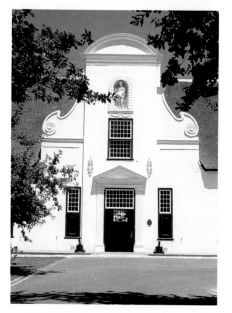

SOUTH AFRICA IS A LAND of majestic landscapes, of endless golden beaches and wide open spaces. It is often described as a land of contrasts, for surely few other countries or even continents can offer so varied an experience as the visitor here is able to have. The contrast between awesome mountain panoramas and frighteningly desolate sweeps of desert; between the bushveld regions of the Transvaal, where wild game roams, and the wave-caressed coral reefs of the Indian Ocean provides a constant string of surprises for those in search of adventure.

The land's tapestry is woven from the subtle, pastel hues of ancient Africa, invigorated by more vivid, geometric designs that man has imposed on the scene relatively recently. Here, modern cultures and primeval nature live, not always harmoniously, side by side. Highways stretch like aluminium strips past tribal dwellings; from the undulating expanses of olive green and khaki-coloured bush, cities rise up like anachronistic building blocks on some outrageously gigantic child's playground.

You can stay in a five-star hotel overlooking Johannesburg's mine dumps or Cape Town's famous Table Mountain, or watch surfers riding the barreling waves on the Indian Ocean. You could fall asleep to the haunting sounds of the African bush, from within the reed and thatch 'boma' of a luxury game lodge. You could even do it the outdoor way, sleeping in rustic mountain chalets along the country's national hiking way system. All these are threads in the same roughly textured topographical cloth.

To experience the country in all its moods and guises would take a lifetime, but with about three weeks in hand, the determined and well-organized traveller could see a great deal. The 'port of entry' would in all probability be Johannesburg. Take a short ride to the 'sin emporium' of Sun City, flagship of southern Africa's hotel industry, and gambling pleasure dome. From here you would want to head east – first into the forest-cloaked, mist-shrouded mountainlands of the Transvaal Escarpment, then to plunge one vertical kilometre into the steamy Lowveld. This is game country: wild African bush that is covered by a patchwork of private and national game reserves, chief of which is the world-renowned Kruger National Park. Do it in style if you choose, by taking the Lowveld Express. The luxuriousness of this steam train journey has been modelled on its famous Orient counterpart.

From here our journey takes us past the tiny mountain kingdom of Swaziland through the rural African areas of Zululand, to Durban, the city that hugs the warm Indian Ocean, and typifies the sunny smile of South Africa. This is where the body worshippers can be found, so catch a tan. Only two hours' drive inland, the mighty Drakensberg, or 'Dragon Mountains', offer spectacular views, forested, waterfall-washed gorges, rock spires, buttresses, and towers that resemble Gothic cathedrals. Accommodation here ranges from luxury hotels, through country inns to mountaineers' chalets. The road south through 'independent' Transkei is long and potentially monotonous, but, for the intrepid traveller prepared to brave some appalling roads, the rewards of the magnificent Wild Coast may well be worth the effort. Alternatively, a short flight to East London or Port Elizabeth will bring

ABOVE *Buskers lend a carnival atmosphere to fleamarkets such as this one in Cape Town's Greenmarket Square. These open-air shopping centres have become a major tourist and general feature of most large cities.* CENTRE *The elegant facade of Groot Constantia, the country's oldest producing wine estate. History, wine tasting, good eating and craft shops make a visit here a must on any tour of the Cape Peninsula.* LEFT *The famous Newlands sports grounds in Cape Town offer a perfect site to launch hot air balloons.*

you to wonderful beaches and warm sea, and a drive to Cape Town along the country's showcard of natural beauty – the Garden Route.

The Garden Route follows the temperate coastline of the south eastern Cape, passing by quaint coastal villages, through forests lorded over by giant yellowwood trees, past the lakeland Wilderness, over spectacular arched bridges that span precipitous ravines. Continuing across the rolling wheatlands of the southern Cape with their backdrop of folded mountains, the road finally winds down tortuous passes to the western Cape coastal plain, but is terminated by Table Mountain and the historic 'mother city' of Cape Town. The western Cape itself is a tourist's wonderland, mixing historical city sights with wild mountain- and sea-scapes, or the cultural gems of the Boland wine farms. If your visit coincides with springtime, the wild-flower displays of northern Namaqualand are a sight not to be missed. Finally, you can take the celebrated five-star Blue Train across the Karoo and Highveld expanses back to Johannesburg.

Many first-time visitors to South Africa are surprised by the sophisticated infrastructure that exists here. On the other hand, it is hard not to be appalled by the poor conditions in which most of the country's black people are forced to live. But it is easy to misinterpret the signs that are boiling within this cultural melting pot. There is always the danger of oversimplifying the complex weave of interacting forces that hold the national garment together.

Although there are some encouraging signs that the country is moving towards a non-discriminatory, more equitable 'deal' for all its people, the white Nationalist Government of the day persists, against growing pressure from within the country and abroad, with the cornerstones of its apartheid policies, insisting that people of different racial groups should live separately and have their own separate political structures within the framework of a central government. By far the largest racial group is the black one numbering around 20 million; Blacks are those peoples who have traditionally lived in Africa. The second biggest racial group is the white one, numbering about five million. Then come the so-called Coloureds – people of mixed black-and-white descent – numbering somewhere in the region of three million, and finally the Asian population of about one million people.

It is a commonly held misconception among many of the country's harshest critics that black South Africans form a homogeneous cultural and political group. Although a broad common purpose in terms of political aspirations can be discerned, there are many cultural and linguistic differences that create conflicts within. Not least of these is the question of traditional 'roots', as many black South Africans are proud of their ancestry – be it Zulu, Xhosa, Sotho, Tswana or Ndebele – and feel a common bond with those who share it. It would also be incorrect to assume that the other groups – the Coloureds, Asians and Whites – form homogeneous groups, for within their ranks opinion, political belief and cultural ties are just as diverse and complex. But complicating the issue even further are the languages people speak. The official languages of South Africa are English and Afrikaans, and an ability to communicate in at least one of these two languages is essential to anybody living in the country. Most South Africans speak these only as second languages, however, and apart from the ten major African languages, there are the many European languages which have been brought here by immigrants, including a 600,000 strong Portuguese community.

ABOVE *Choose jazz or folk music, driving rock 'n roll, or perhaps a gentle ballad to serenade a meal and a drink.* CENTRE *The University of Cape Town maintains high academic standards in all fields, but is probably best known for its medical faculty at Groote Schuur Hospital where the world's first heart transplant operation was performed by Professor Christiaan Barnard.* RIGHT *The beaches of South Africa are among the best in the world and sun-worshippers abound during the long, hot summers.*

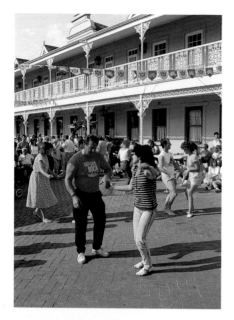

Following the discovery of large diamond and gold deposits a century ago, and more recently uranium, iron, coal, manganese, copper and many other precious metals, South Africa was the first country on the African continent to become highly industrialized. The formal economy exists alongside a more traditional market economy of the black rural areas, as well as an informal sector in the economically depressed black urban areas. Some people see the socio-economic disparity between the country's First and Third World elements as an exploitative relationship, while others see it as a bold and dynamic social experiment, the symbiosis of two basically different cultures – a meeting of northern and southern hemispheres.

It is generally the more technologically advanced countries, those that have already traded much of their natural resources for material wealth, that are today the most conservation-minded. In this regard South Africa can be counted as technologically advanced, yet is unique in that, due to the fore-sightedness of some of its founders, it retains so much of its wildlife resources.

On a continent whose remaining wildlife resources are besieged, and being plundered to a horrific degree, South Africa remains steadfast in its fight for conservation and the protection of endangered species. In the cases of both the square-lipped and the hook-lipped rhinoceroses (white and black respectively), for instance, this country maintains a breeding programme that serves as a healthy gene pool and a reservoir for the stocking of other wildlife areas in southern Africa.

In the western Cape Province is found the smallest of the world's six floral kingdoms. The Cape Peninsula is about the size of the Isle of Wight, yet it alone contains more plant species than the entire British Isles. For centuries, the western Cape has delighted visitors and astounded botanists and taxonomists with the amazing diversity of its flowering plants.

Because of the typically small, tightly folded leaves of many of the plants here, the Dutch settlers coined the term 'fynbos' (fine bush). Today this term is considered to be botanically limiting, but it is still generally used to refer to the proteas, orchids and ericas, the pelargoniums and gladioluses, the reed-like restios and thousands of other plants that flower through all seasons.

Perhaps it was prophetic that one of the names given to the Cape by the Portuguese sailors who passed it on their way to the East during the 15th, 16th and 17th centuries was *Cabo Tormentoso,* or Cape of Storms. In a few hundred years the social scene at the southern tip of Africa was to change from fairly simple, to one of the most complex and dynamic in history.

When Jan van Riebeeck, leader of the first Dutch settlers to the Cape, arrived there in 1652 the only inhabitants were Khoikhoi (Hottentot) herders and 'strandlopers', or beachcombers. Further inland, the colonists made scant contact with the elusive San (Bushmen) nomads, who at that time wandered in small hunter-gatherer clans across most of southern Africa.

Van Riebeeck's party was sent to establish a halfway refreshment station between the Netherlands and Batavia, the former country's trading headquarters in the East. From tentative beginnings on the shores of what Sir Francis Drake is reputed to have called 'the fairest Cape in all the circumference of the world', grew the city of Cape Town. In 1688 the small colony was invigorated by the arrival of about 200 French Huguenot refugees. These were Protestants who had fled Catholic persecution after the Edict of Nantes had been revoked. They settled in the beautiful Boland, or 'up-

ABOVE *At a disused mine in Johannesburg, an old gold rush town has been re-created. Here at Gold Reef City entertainment is a 24-hour business.* CENTRE *Johannesburg - the city that was built on gold. The Johannesburg Sun Hotel (foreground) is one of the many luxury hotels found throughout the country.* LEFT *As in so many countries, football (or soccer) is a national sport in South Africa. Despite it being banned from the international arena, enthusiasm runs high and local trophies are fiercely contested.*

country', valley now named Franschhoek (Dutch for 'French corner') where they set about building magnificent gabled homesteads and refining the fledgling wine industry at this remote European outpost.

Today these Boland wine farms are among the country's most prosperous agricultural enterprises, especially since the wines themselves have truly come of age, holding their own with the best in the world. The historic estates, set among the fissured crags of the Cape Folded Mountains, are one of the country's most prestigious tourist attractions.

During the early 19th century, the Cape was forcibly taken from the Dutch by the British. The advent of Europe's industrial revolution created unemployment in the United Kingdom and forced thousands to seek new lives in 'the colonies'. The arrival of the 1820 Settlers at the Cape added a new dimension to the colony's developing human tapestry. They were placed along the Cape's troubled eastern frontier, as a buffer against the southward-advancing Xhosa people. In many ways these settlers had a liberalizing effect on the local political fabric, much as did their kind in North America.

The Dutch farmers at the Cape never took kindly to British domination, particularly their decision to abolish slavery, and trekked first eastwards along the coast, and then northwards as a defiant act of independence. Finally, in the mid-1830s, thousands of Boer (farmer) families packed their meagre belongings into sturdy ox wagons and headed off into the African hinterland in search of their own 'promised land'. These Voortrekkers (pioneers), who were the moving spirit in the formation of the Afrikaans-speaking population, were Calvinists of deep conviction. They firmly believed that they were one of God's chosen people, and set off in search of a new Canaan.

But these independent-minded breakaways did nothing to please the British imperialists, especially since they blocked the road for further British colonial expansion into Africa. No sooner had the British forcibly annexed the Boer republic of Natal, than diamonds and gold – in great quantities – were unearthed in land claimed by the Voortrekkers.

By this stage both parties were spoiling for a fight, and when war was officially declared in 1899, each confidently believed that it would defeat the other by Christmas. In fact, the war lasted for three bitter years, costing the British Empire its heaviest victory ever, and levying from the Boers their land, many of their best men, women and children, and their very dream of freedom and independence. Still today, the scars from the Anglo-Boer War are evident in the estrangement and mistrust that divides English- and Afrikaans-speaking South Africans.

Up until about thirty years before the Voortrekkers pushed northwards into the African hinterland, most of the northern and eastern interior of southern Africa had been occupied for some centuries by a relatively stable Iron-age culture of black pastoralists. But, by this time, the ever-expanding populations who occupied the country's principal grazing lands, began to cause tribes to crowd each other. From the beginning of the 19th century powerful warlords emerged among them, conquering and consolidating all the lesser tribes that lived in the interior. Most significant of these was Shaka, founder and first king of the Zulu nation. Shaka was a merciless ruler and a brilliant military tactician, who was dubbed 'the black Napoleon'.

By 1820 several prominent warlords faced each other across the grassveld and mountainous expanses. For a decade their 'impis', or regimented

ABOVE *Mine dancing, a mixture of tribal rhythms and city beat, is a popular attraction for visitors to the Johannesburg area.* CENTRE *Sun City in neighbouring Bophuthatswana is a hotel/entertainment complex where gambling and rock concerts, dancing extravaganzas and the world's most lucrative golf classic are regular events.* RIGHT *The ethnic cultures of black South Africans are richly imbued with a delight for adornment and decoration. Rural Ndebele people show a strong preference for vividly-coloured geometric patterns.*

15

warriors, engaged in ferocious wars that laid waste this once peaceful, pastoral area. These *Difaquane* wars were followed by widespread droughts that contributed to the decimation of the tribes living north and west of the Drakensberg Escarpment. To the east of the Escarpment lived the highly militarized and proud Zulus, against whom the Voortrekkers waged many bloody battles – gunpowder and lead against stabbing spears and cow-hide shields – eventually subduing them at the Battle of Blood River. But it was only after later wars against the British Army, and later through crippling taxes and land legislation, that the military power of the Zulus was broken.

All these events drove the country's black people to seek work on white-owned farms, and later in the mines and supporting industries. When peace was signed between Boer and Briton in 1902, the Boers managed to delay British plans to extend the voting franchise to all South Africans. When the Union of South Africa was formed in 1910, they once again bargained to keep politics an all-white affair.

Slavery was a fundamental part of the development of the Cape colony. The small number of Hottentots were never willing servants, so the Dutch imported slaves, mainly from East Africa, Madagascar and the Netherlands' territories in the East, to carry out all manual labour. There was a fair degree of mixing between white colonists, freed slaves, the Khoikhoi and various black people where these cultures met and from these associations were born the country's three million Coloureds, a group of great diversity, although the descendants of those who came from the East Indies, the Cape Malays, have retained a strong identity through their Islamic faith and culture.

After colonization the British settlers turned most of Natal's lush, subtropical coastal bushveld into undulating sugar cane plantations. To work in the cane fields, they brought in indentured labourers from India. When their contracts were up, the Indians were offered either a free passage home or title to a plot of Crown Land. Most chose to stay, forming the 'Asian' population of South Africa.

After the two world wars, South Africa welcomed a flood of immigrants from the devastation of war-torn Europe; later, during the decolonization of Africa in the 1960's and '70s, 'sunny South Africa' received a wave of expatriot refugees who chose to remain in Africa rather than return to Europe.

And yet, before the white people, before even the black people lived here, South Africa was inhabited by the San (Bushmen), they who called themselves the 'first people'. The San had few material possessions and a rich mythical and spiritual life. But these children of nature were essentially hunter-gatherers who roamed the veld taking only what they needed; white farmers could not tolerate their wild ways, and so they were shot like vermin.

First they were pushed into the Drakensberg mountains, and finally into the western deserts. It is now only in the Kalahari thirstland, beyond South African borders, that San survive in small numbers. But, in the caves that pock the Drakensberg's sandstone base, their shamans painted the walls with animal, human and mythical figures. This legacy of cave paintings has been called the greatest art gallery in the world.

Who lived here before the San, no-one knows, but some of the earliest hominid remains have been found in South Africa. In caves around the country fossils of various upright but pre-human primates gave palaeontologists their first glimmer of light as they peered into the darkness

ABOVE *A young girl in rural Transkei. The so-called independent republics of Transkei and Ciskei lie either side of East London and are home to the majority of Xhosa-speaking people.* CENTRE *One of the finest examples of colonial-style buildings that hail from the period of British administration in South Africa, is Pietermaritzburg's town hall.* LEFT *Once a year a sardine run occurs along the Natal coast. Here fishermen congregate on the shores of the St. Lucia nature reserve in Zululand, casting for the game fish that follow the sardines.*

that shrouds mankind's past. These australopithecines lived in sub-Saharan Africa around 2,5 million years ago. It seems they were the first creatures to harness the power of fire, and to use crude stone tools.

That man was born in sub-Saharan Africa is now beyond dispute. But in rocks of the semi-arid Karoo region, once a vast inland sea, those horizontal strata that give South Africa its characteristic wide openness, there has been found the longest unbroken record of prehistoric life. From the wealth of Karoo fossils scientists have pieced together an awe-inspiring tale: from the first primitive amphibian that crawled out of a Palaeozoic ocean, through the emergence of gargantuan mammal-like reptiles, to the appearance of a rabbit-sized mammal some 50 million years later.

To many people rocks are simply rocks, and landscapes are, well, landscapes, but what incredible stories they have to tell to anyone who takes the time to listen. The Drakensberg, the highest and youngest mountains in southern Africa, are some 200 million years old. Comparatively, the Himalayas, the Andes and the Rockies are all geological adolescents. South Africa is truly an ancient landscape; the languid night air over the savanna bushveld vibrates with the rhythms of primeval Africa, and its soil and rock encase secrets that tell of life's very beginnings.

All South Africans harbour a deep passion for this land, a passion bred of its immensity and beauty. Perhaps it is this passion that is at the root of the country's political conflict. For South Africans are passionate about politics too. Apartheid, the policy of racial segregation and the creation of tribal 'homelands', was the brain-child of the Nationalist Party; a mightily miscalculated effort to resolve the country's political divisions. Because its motives were based in continued white domination, it was, as evinced by current happenings, doomed to die, albeit slowly.

When one thinks of South Africa's main cities one immediately thinks of Johannesburg, Pretoria, Cape Town and Durban. But the most populous city in South Africa is all-black Soweto, and yet it has no central business district, no industry to speak of, no large department stores or fashionable boutiques. As one of apartheid's cornerstones, the country's Group Areas Act declares that people of different skin colour shall not live in the same areas. Therefore every white town and city has a black alter ego, a dormitory town that serves the labour needs of its white counterpart.

Cities like Soweto are an ever-present reminder of the divided nation of South African society and will continue as such well into the future, irrespective of how the politics of the country will resolve. But in many ways people are beginning to come together as South Africans working for a common future.

No sensible person could deny that South Africa faces many challenges, and just how these should be met is the source of much heated debate at home and abroad. It is a country made up of people of different backgrounds and cultural values, but it is this very diversity that is at once its dilemma and also its great potential. On one thing, though, there is general accord – South Africa is a beautiful corner of the world and well lives up to the marketing boast of 'a world in one country'. The traveller faces an almost limitless choice of what to do and see: sophisticated cities, first-class hotels, beautiful scenery, sun-drenched beaches and, above all, a wildlife and floral heritage that is unparalleled anywhere in the world.

ABOVE *The colourful flower market outside Durban's town hall which is a replica of that in Belfast, Northern Ireland.* CENTRE *Bloemfontein's imposing Raadsaal, the parliament of the old, somewhat shortlived (1854-1900) Orange Free State republic. In front stands the equestrian statue of General Christiaan de Wet, the famed guerrilla leader and one of the Boer heroes of the Anglo-Boer War of 1899-1902.* RIGHT *The Workshop, part of the old station complex in Durban, has found new life as a vibrant shopping centre.*

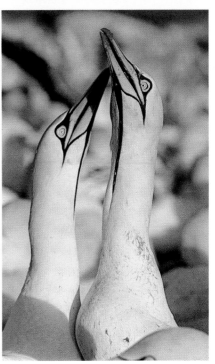

LEFT *The springtime flowering spectacle that bursts out across the arid Namaqualand plains each year is, ironically, a measure of the area's environmental degradation. Although they would occur naturally, these plants act as pioneer species; where overgrazing is worst, the annual bloom will be most impressive, especially when the winter rains have been good.*

ABOVE *Mesembryanthemums - a vivid splash of purple in the springtime carpet.*

TOP RIGHT *With the over-exploitation of pelagic fish off Africa's south-western Cape coast, fishermen tend to accuse Cape fur seals of 'stealing' their catches. In a well-balanced ecosystem, where man takes only that share that allows for the resource to naturally renew itself, there would be enough for the fishermen, the seals and sharks alike.*

ABOVE RIGHT *The small islands off the south-western coast are home to dense breeding colonies of sea birds, such as these Cape gannets. The islands have for centuries supported a guano industry, where once a year the phosphorous-rich deposits are scraped off the rocks and used for fertilizer.*

LEFT *Jan van Riebeeck, the founding father of Cape Town, would surely be surprised if he could see how the settlement has grown, from a tiny victualling station in 1652 to mother city of the nation. Cape Town nestles in a bowl between the sea, Table Mountain (shown here) and the flanking prominences of Devil's Peak and Lion's Head.*

TOP *Table Mountain is possibly the world's most climbed peak, with a network of paths and rock climbing routes criss-crossing its every aspect. Most visitors prefer to take the cableway to the top, from which the views of the city and Table Bay are magnificent. Often, as the cable car heads for the upper station, rock climbers can be seen inching their way up the cliffs directly below.*

ABOVE *Cape Town came into being as a halfway station for sailing ships travelling between Europe and the East. When the Suez canal was opened the port lost its strategic significance, except for a brief period during the 1960s when political instability in the Middle East allowed the 'tavern of the seas' to relive its heyday.*

ABOVE *Cape Point, variously known as the Cape of Storms or the Cape of Good Hope - depending on whether you were actually sailing around it or whether you were trying to persuade seafarers of old to sail around it. A popular myth would have people believe that the Atlantic and Indian oceans meet off the Point; in reality no such meeting takes place and, if it did, it would occur far beyond the horizon.*

LEFT *The beaches of Clifton, where the country's trendsetting sun-worshippers play. Real Estate abutting the beach is among the most sought after in the country.*

LEFT ABOVE *Llandudno, a charming suburban cove on the outskirts of Cape Town. In summertime the chilly upwelled water of the Atlantic Ocean causes the surf temperature to drop as low as 10 °C, but the locals are used to it and flock to this superb, wind-free beach.*

OVERLEAF *The Cape of Good Hope, not to be confused with adjoining Cape Point, was where Bartolomeu Dias landed in 1488 and planted a stone cross on his pioneering sea voyage from Portugal.*

LEFT ABOVE *The Kirstenbosch National Botanical Gardens are the pride of local horticulturists and botanists, where glorious displays of indigenous flowers, shrubs and trees create a floral wonderland. Up the east-facing slopes of Table Mountain, the gardens blend into the natural Afro-montane forests that festoon the mountain. This is a rambler's paradise.*

FAR LEFT *A pair of black eagles. These majestic raptors are commonly found in mountainous areas throughout southern Africa, where they thrill climbers and hikers with their exciting aerial displays.*

LEFT *One of mankind's close relatives, a chacma baboon, savours a flower. Like humans, baboons are versatile creatures that can survive in just about any environment providing water is available.*

ABOVE *A species of* Selago *and protea bloom (right), just two of the plants that make up the Cape's famous plant life. The variety and diversity of flowering plants in the Western Cape has led botanists to declare this tiny area one of the world's six floral kingdoms.*

Stellenbosch, heartland of the country's wine industry. As the Cape Colony expanded, this was the first settlement established by the Dutch colonists in the area still referred to as the 'Boland' or hinterland. It lies barely 40 km east of Cape Town.

TOP *The gabled facade of the historical Boschendal homestead, one of the finest examples of Cape Dutch architecture to be found. The estate's wine cellars and its superb buffet restaurant are open to the public for most of the year.*

ABOVE *Most of the country's wine farms are situated in fertile valleys that lie between the parallel crags of what geologists call the Cape Folded Mountains. Among the most beautiful of all these settings is Franschhoek, where 200 French Huguenots settled just over 300 years ago. Today the Franschhoek association of vignerons carries on the making of fine wines in the French tradition.*

ABOVE *The Karoo sprawls across about two-thirds of the South African interior. It is a more or less flat, semi-arid region that owes its character to the horizontally bedded series of rocks of the area. Fossils found in these rocks reveal an unbroken record of evolution spanning over 50 million years; as such it is one of the country's, and the world's, great natural wonders.*

RIGHT *From a viewing point just outside the Karoo town of Graaff-Reinet, one looks out over the pale landscape of what the Khoi Hottentots called the Plains of Camdeboo. White settlers, crossing the blazing, sandy expanse in ox wagons, called it the Valley of Desolation.*

LEFT *The mighty Augrabies Falls on the Orange River. Over the ages the mighty waters have driven great boulders to carve deep potholes at the bottom of which are reported to lie a vast wealth in alluvial diamonds. The falls lie within the Augrabies Falls National Park.*

ABOVE *Throughout the country's arid western region, burrowing ground squirrels can be seen sitting on their haunches by the roadside.*

ABOVE RIGHT *A spotted eagle owl sits silently on a gravel road, its nocturnally attuned eyes flaring in the photographer's flashlight.*

LEFT *and* ABOVE *Just to the north of Johannesburg and Pretoria in neighbouring Bophuthatswana, is the pleasure dome of Sun City, a lush hotel, entertainment and sports complex that is landscaped out of the veld. Although not everyone's cup of tea, Sun City is undeniably impressive and the gardens are a masterpiece. To create this horticultural paradise, huge natural rocks and massive, mature forest trees were brought to the site.*

OVERLEAF *Jacaranda trees, although not indigenous, are a favourite garden tree in South Africa. Pretoria, other than being the country's executive capital, is known as the 'jacaranda city'. Most streets are lined with jacarandas, and each spring they delight with showers of mauve blossoms.*

ABOVE *A short drive from Pretoria is the Hartebeestpoort Dam which lies along the foot of the Magaliesberg Mountains. For the land-locked urban complex of Johannesburg and Pretoria, this is a popular recreation spot.*

ABOVE *To the uninitiated observer, the Magaliesberg range looks little more than a line of unimpressive hills. But the ancient forces that formed them also cut a network of sheer gorges deep into the quartzite, where rivers cascade and wild animals find refuge. Rock climbers, birdwatchers, archaeologists, hikers and all manner of nature lovers delight in these secluded retreats.*

LEFT *With spinnaker flying, a yacht slices through the fresh waters of Loch Vaal. This man-made reservoir on the Vaal River is the principle source of water for the Pretoria-Johannesburg-Vereeniging industrial complex.*

ABOVE *Egoli, the African name for Johannesburg, the city of gold and hub of South Africa's business world. Barely 100 years ago the first diggers' shacks were placed tentatively on the open grassy plains of the wild African veld. No-one then could have realized the extent of the wealth that lay beneath them or that their tent-town would become one of the great metropolises of Africa.*

LEFT *In the heart of Johannesburg's prestigious northern suburbs, Zoo Lake and its surrounds offer a tranquil respite from the rigours of frenetic city life.*

ABOVE *and* RIGHT *Magoebaskloof in the Eastern Transvaal. Between the oppressive heat, the flies, malaria-carrying mosquitoes and wild animals of the Lowveld, and the temperate grasslands of the Highveld, lies the Eastern Transvaal Escarpment - a mist-shrouded mountainland that is one of the country's most popular tourist attractions. Prevailing winds from the Indian Ocean push their rain-laden clouds up against the escarpment, where natural forests and timber plantations flourish.*

PREVIOUS PAGE *After a heavy downpour, sunlight bursts through dark clouds to bathe the Blyde River Canyon in soft light. A popular five-day hiking trail, one of many that make up a national hiking way network, follows the rim of this spectacular gorge.*

ABOVE *At the foot of the Eastern Transvaal Escarpment lies the Lowveld. This is big game country and home to the famous Kruger National Park, as well as a host of private reserves and lodges. Here where the struggle for survival is tangible, animals have evolved many ingenious defence mechanisms. The stark geometric lines of a zebra's hide, for instance, provide excellent camouflage in the dappled light of a savanna's tree and grass mosaic.*

TOP *Although many other animals have more fearsome reputations, hippopotamuses are by nature moody, and along the country's east-flowing rivers they account for at least as many human deaths as do crocodiles.*

ABOVE *The formidable Nile crocodile can weigh as much as 1 000 kilograms and although fish are the basis of its diet, humans are regularly taken as well as game. Even zebra and buffalo may be overcome by this primitive reptile.*

LEFT ABOVE *Lions have a special aura and certainly no visit to the game-rich Lowveld would be complete without seeing these supreme African predators. Lions spend about 80 per cent of their time sleeping, but when roused and on the hunt their power is truly awesome, as evidenced by this downing of a wildebeest.*

LEFT *Hyaenas are widely thought of as repulsive carrion feeders, but recent studies have shown these so-called scavengers to be more successful hunters than lions.*

ABOVE *Leopards are for the most part solitary hunters with well-defined territories. Because of their secretive, mostly nocturnal behaviour, they have managed to survive in areas where all other large carnivores have long since been exterminated.*

LEFT *and* TOP *Big tuskers like these are prize targets for ivory poachers, and hence few survive. In the protected environment of the Kruger National Park, however, there is a relatively large population of bull elephants with large tusks. Elephants may be reputed to be slow, poor-sighted creatures, but they move with surprising speed and should always be treated with great respect, even from the relative safety of a motor vehicle.*

ABOVE LEFT *The real jewels of the African Bushveld are its birdlife. Once familiar with the larger animals, it is sightings such as this whitefronted bee-eater that delight many visitors to the country's game parks.*

ABOVE RIGHT *The bateleur eagle is a masterful flier and its eye-catching black and red markings make it all the more striking.*

OPPOSITE ABOVE *Buffaloes are easily identified by their huge, low-slung horns. Their placid appearance belies their often irritable nature; a wounded buffalo is reputed to be a hunter's most feared quarry.*

OPPOSITE BELOW *When it comes to hunting, size will often determine the strategy that a predator adopts. Wild dogs are relatively small, but because they hunt in family groups, they are perhaps the most proficient predators in Africa.*

ABOVE *Brindled gnus are more commonly known as blue wildebeest, a name given them by early Dutch settlers, who tended to see these animals as 'wild cattle'.*

LEFT *This dwarf species is one of 10 mongooses found in South Africa. The dwarf mongoose is active during the day when it feeds mainly on insects as well as the eggs of ground-nesting birds and snakes.*

PREVIOUS PAGE *Few sights are as thrilling as a herd of impala, in full flight, bounding and leaping. Honed to physical perfection by what Charles Darwin termed 'the struggle for survival', these elegant antelopes can leap a distance of 12 metres with apparent ease.*

OPPOSITE *It is often said jokingly that the Orange Free State is so flat that one can see tomorrow coming down the road, and yet the province's north-eastern border with Lesotho is a scenic mountainland. The Brandwag, or Sentinel (shown here), is one of the spectacular sandstone formations from which the Golden Gate Highlands National Park derives its name.*

ABOVE *When autumn spreads its frosty gown over the Highveld, the land retaliates with a brave display of cosmos blooms. These exotic flowers were introduced to the country at the turn of the century during the Second Anglo-Boer War, as seeds in the fodder for British horses.*

ABOVE *The Amphitheatre, one of the most frequently painted and photographed Drakensberg scenes. The mighty Drakensberg range is South Africa's best known mountain area and is visited by thousands of people every year .*

RIGHT *The magnificent bearded vulture or lammergeier is an endangered species in southern Africa, found only in the Drakensberg mountains and in Lesotho.*

OPPOSITE *The view towards Devil's Tooth, part of the Amphitheatre's Eastern Buttress. Nineteenth century Boer pioneers gave the range its present name, Drakensberg, meaning dragon mountains. Early Zulus gave these basalt spires the more poetic name of* Quathlamba - *the barrier of spears.*

TOP *Between Champagne Castle (left) and Cathkin Peak (right), is the free-standing Monk's Cowl, which has claimed the lives of more rock climbers than any other peak in the Drakensberg.*

ABOVE *The Horns, The Bell and Cathedral Peak loom above the Mlambonja Valley.*

LEFT *The Drakensberg foothills are a garden of natural delights. Navarone Dam in the Garden Castle area is typical of the 'Little Berg's' attractions.*

PREVIOUS PAGE *From its marshy spring, set a kilometre back from the Escarpment edge, the Tugela River commences its seaward journey by cascading over the Amphitheatre in three mighty leaps.*

ABOVE *Countless mountain-fresh streams and rivers rush through the Little Berg foothills - and many of them are filled with trout. These freshwater game fish do not naturally occur here, but the rivers have long been stocked. There is currently a conflict between conservationists and fly fishermen, for whom their sport is more important than indigenous species being eaten out by the voracious trout.*

LEFT *In the gentle Natal Midlands, where many of the country's 'gentleman farmers' may be found, the Howick Falls punctuate the Mgeni River, which flows into the Indian Ocean just north of Durban.*

LEFT *A lone surfer against the backdrop of a threatening storm and Durban's skyline of beachfront hotels. Durban's subtropical climate makes it a year-round holiday mecca with hundreds of thousands of people, mainly from inland Transvaal and Orange Free State, flocking to the fine beaches of Natal that extend from the city along the north and south coasts.*

ABOVE *The tranquil haven of Durban's Point Yacht Club.*

ABOVE *A few hours' drive north of Durban is Lake St Lucia, in reality not a lake but an estuary which lies within a nature reserve. The St Lucia complex has much to offer, especially the nature lover as it has large crocodile and hippo populations, wild game along the shores and a most spectacular diversity of wetland bird species.*

OPPOSITE ABOVE *The Natal Parks Board has, in its Zululand reserves, developed breeding herds of both white and black rhinoceroses. The 'white' species, seen here in the Umfolozi Game Reserve, is a grazer, whereas its so-called 'black' cousin is strictly a browser.*

OPPOSITE BELOW *Although the bushveld savanna stretches in a narrowing wedge down through Natal and into the Eastern Cape, most of the large game species occurring in this habitat, such as Burchell's zebra (shown here), are found no further south than Zululand's game reserves.*

RIGHT *Wherever there are wild waterways in Africa the haunting shriek of the fish eagle can be heard. These birds hunt by swooping down on fish and snatching them in their powerful talons. Then, with wings struggling to gain lift, they rise with a catch weighing anything up to four kilograms.*

ABOVE *Plettenberg Bay and the estuary of the Bietou River. This peaceful scene belies the bustling activity of the nearby town of the same name. Once a sleepy seaside settlement, Plettenberg Bay is now the focus of the many holiday makers that flock to the Garden Route at every opportunity.*

RIGHT *An aerial view of the Bloukrans River as it cuts a swathe through the forest. Deep gorges such as this are common along the Garden Route, and bridging them has presented many a challenge to the skills of civil engineers.*

OPPOSITE *The mouth of the Storms River in the Tsitsikamma Coastal National Park. It is here that the Otter Trail begins - a tough but extremely popular four-day hike along the rugged, tree-lined coastline.*